A GIFT FOR YOUR JOURNEY

A Book About Loss and Greater Gain

BY LINDA STRAIT

A Gift For Your Journey
© 2020 by Linda Strait

All rights reserved. No part of this book may be used or reproduced in any manner whatsoever, including internet usage, without written permission from Linda Strait, except in the case of brief quotations embodied in critical articles and reviews.

ISBN: 978-1-7347706-2-9 (paperback)
ISBN: 978-1-7347706-4-3 (hardback)
ISBN: 978-1-7347706-3-6 (ebook)

Library of Congress Number
2 0 2 0 9 1 0 0 7 9

First Edition, 2020
The Publishing Portal 2020
www.thepublishingportal.com

DEDICATION

This book is dedicated to those seeking more joy in their life. To those who know that life can be better. To those who are willing to look with honest, open eyes at changing their own patterns, to create the life that they seek. It's hand-holding time. You are not alone. Ever.

PREFACE

Once I was awakened, I had to accept my personal power. I had spent so much time seeking a guru, savior, guide—someone who would take me under his or her wing and say "I will show you the way." Awakening meant that I realized no one would be doing that. I am responsible for myself. I make choices by myself, for myself. There was no one else to lean on. Yes, there is much help available. It is true that I was not truly alone (none of us ever are!), but my choices had to come from me alone. I had to _own_ them, and that was scary.

I will tell you, my beautiful friends, that there is no other way to build trust within yourself. And trusting yourself leads to loving yourself. And that is your ticket out of the confusing mazes that we have all built.

I am sharing some poems from my journey with you. My intent in doing so is to give you encouragement and help you realize that you are not alone. I want you to know how brave you are. Your courage is recognized. Don't back down. You are _so_ worth it!

Since you are here with me, I know that you are paying attention to the very personal longing within you for a more joy-filled, authentic life. We are all at different places in this process, each of us unique, but we are all on this journey home together. Join me as my spiritual family in coming to a place of joy, peace and love. I am so glad to be with you!

I would love to hear from you as we build our community of truth seekers and joy finders. Let's get to know each other.

Love,
Linda

Touch

I want to touch you with my words—
with the feelings they evoke
To bring you back to that innocent, connected space
when you didn't question everything
When you trusted and believed and took it all in.
This touch of mine
Wraps you in love like your Grandmother's shawl;
Hugs you tightly,
Like your Fathers strong arms;
Looks deeply into your eyes and brings you the safety of your
Mother's lap.
As you deserve without earning
If you go deeply within you'll find peace there—
passed all of the scary nightmares that you came to believe.
Shed them off—Throw them away
And join me in this journey of finding the true you--
The you that others could not see because of *their* wounds.
You are truly beautiful and …
I love you so!

I Know a Secret

I know a Secret
It should not be so
It should be shouted from the rooftops
and taught in every classroom.
It is a great truth
And truths are to be revealed and lived and become a part of your foundation.
not buried and covered up never to be spoken of

The secret is this:
YOU are Loved
YOU are perfect
YOU ARE.
The lie that we have allowed to flourish
is that all things are not from Love.
You are not enough. There is not enough
Time for a major cleaning
Open the windows
Roll up your sleeves
Start at the basement and work your way up
Until you GLOW with the Light of Love
And all else has been recognized as dust.

WHY?

What am I missing because I don't ask why?
What assumptions keep me blind?
Wisdom has to be invited to penetrate walls
Seekers have to be willing to be exposed.

Hiding in Plain Sight

Holding your breath and hoping the pain will go away—
Don't look at it!
Don't speak it!
Is like hiding by putting a paper bag over your head.

What's It All About?

What's It All About—
this story that you are living?
Thank God you don't know—*can't* know.
It's being revealed as you live it.
Look closely.
Observe as if you were studying for a big test
with an awareness that lets you breathe it in.
Then choose moment to moment
holding each decision to the light of Your Truth.

Pretending

I know what it's like to deny yourself
In order to fit in.
It can't be maintained
Day after day of pretending to be OK with it all
When inside your dialog gets louder
And finally bursts forth into Truth revealed.
Your Truth.
Now you are getting somewhere.
It feels so good to say "No!"
"That's not Ok with me and I won't keep still.
I cannot ignore what I feel any longer.
And now, it's my turn.
You will know My Truth."
And you surprise everyone—even yourself
With your deep conviction
And life gets better, as it falls apart
As the cracks open
Hope is there waiting to lead you in a new direction
And your heart smiles.

Tears

So cleansing
Sob-racking shaking loose of the long held fears
Shame coming to the surface of not being right
Not doing things right
Not being enough
For another.
If I could tell you one thing so that you would take it into your cells
it would be this:
You are not here to live for another and their needs and prejudices.
You are here for yourself
uncovering your God-given perfection
And that's all you need to do.

I Know About Fear

I know the fear.
I know the multi-layered I can't, won't and never!
It is false and stifling.
So I peel them away one by one.
No more self-inflicted wounding
Instead, I found a delicious, beautiful light that danced and twirled and
lifted my Spirit
And I was better for it.
Those protective veils and layers that I built
had gotten in my way.
At one time they made me feel safe,
but, then, I became their prisoner.
I grew up and out and expanded
and I am so much better for it!
I would Love to share that feeling with you
For YOU
Love,
Me

Blinders

There are no pills that you can take
to ease the pain of your emotions
No potions, diets, lifestyle changes
will satisfy what you refuse to hear
Have you noticed?
It's getting louder
May as well sit down and allow

How Do You Feel?

Have you ever had someone tell you how you feel--
As if they knew better than you?
How could they know?
Unless you've buried yourself for so long
that *you* don't even know how you feel.
You are so out of touch with your own heart
that others can mold you to their liking.
This is not the life God meant for you.
You've simply wandered away from your source.
Time to go back.

You'll Never Amount to Anything

You'll never amount to anything…
Damaging words so easily spoken
embedded in my mind.
You think that I forgot—kids do, you say
but what may not have been in my surface memory
was in my cells.
It affected my life—my choices—my willingness to take risks—
my belief in myself.
It has come to me later in life
just how much your words hurt me.
I finally recognize the lie.
I am inherently valuable—
a product of God's creation.
I don't have to earn anything, prove anything…to you.

I know three things:
Your words were about you—not me.
When my search for joy became strong,
your words became my motivation.
And finally, they brought me to a place of forgiveness
First for you, then for me.
That hurt child within me is now solidly, confidently, within my heart
Receiving love.
And now I can say
Thank you.

Secrets and Lies

Secrets and Lies--
no base to build your life upon.
Houses tumbling down,
Foundations crumbling;
Damaged beyond repair.
You may think you got away with it
But not so---not so.
Your trustworthiness tarnished black
Those misled, if they are aware,
Go on to build new, stronger houses
But those telling the lies, keeping secrets
must abandon their houses altogether,
Clean up their Earth—the very basest part of them;
the place where you plant your feet
and build a new foundation.
What will you choose this time?
What experience will be yours?
Sand? Limestone?
Or the deepest, purist fertile soil settled on
Solid rock.

No Escape

What do you do when there is no escape?
When your screams are so scorchingly hot
that they don't make a sound?
You become ash---
You give up everything but the most basic dust
And your silent cry
SAVE ME

I Trusted You

I trusted that you loved me
and with the innocence of the child that I was
I followed you into your hell.
It became my hell.
Innocence-- gone.
Knowing what love is--gone.
Feeling safe –gone.
In a matter of minutes you took away my foundation,
destroyed my compass
And left me in a state of panic that settled in
below the surface of my brightly manufactured smile.
Life went on
But I was broken
My ability to trust others and myself---broken.
I was exposed to evil masquerading as love
and was forever changed.
Denial came to my rescue.
In a world that no longer made sense
I could go on.
But the innate desire to give and receive love had a voice that
wouldn't be still.

It saved me, although it was decades before I recognized "saved".
The missteps on my journey to love were building blocks
that kept me asking: "What am I learning from this?"
My divergent pathways kept returning to *me.*
Experiences were determined to bring me to loving *myself;*
Trusting *myself;*
Believing in *myself.*
My willingness to dig deeply—exposing my primal fears,
brought me to a place of forgiveness.
It's been the hardest thing I've ever done…
But oh, so worth it.
I know who I am now.
My compass is back.
My foundation is solid.
And I never ever have to walk that road again.

Silence, Peace

Deep within where cares are laid to rest,
I find a peace that often eludes me.
It's where I rest my mind, like taking off a much-worn pair of shoes
and putting them aside
I allow my heart to speak
Mind over matter
Heart over mind
The wisdom was there all along.
Wisdom that waits for stillness;
Wisdom that refuses to talk over other voices--
often in the form of a whisper.
It lets you know
there is a power there
greater than your understanding,
that leaves you feeling deeply reverent
not wanting to break the silence

Deep Within

There is a place deep within
that is other-worldly.
I go there often. I'd like to stay.
I find that little matters of my daily toils.

Never Give Up

Never give up on yourself!
Be front and center in the investment of you
That means that you don't allow another to take **YOU** down to
an unrecognizable *you* that they brush off like dandruff.
Instead, you nurture your most treasured thoughts--
Knowing that with polishing,
they will shine as you imagine.
Roadblocks are merely things to step over—walk around
They are put there to strengthen your determination to move
forward.
When you are ready
There will be no stopping you.
You will know and accept that there is nothing more important for
you to do
than honor yourself and your visions.
It's God's work.
The world is ready and waiting to accept you with open arms
Welcome my beautiful friend!

Finding Everland

It's there if you look…Don't give up!
It's not hiding.
You have built elaborate mazes that circle and cut through places
never meant to be visited.
Diverting, Complicating,
What could be a simple journey.
Try a path.
If you don't like it,
try another and another and another.
You choose. It's always your choice.
But *how* you labor to place the responsibility elsewhere!
Stop where you are.
Just stop and do nothing
until calmness feeds your soul
And Light becomes YOU.

Victim No More

I refuse to be a victim…
It brings me no joy.
It is a disempowered way of being that **_I do not want_**.
I know the feelings:
It comes as sadness, deflating me and making me small
It comes as anger, stopping me in my tracks while I indulge in the mindset of unfairness
I do not need to stay here.
With the strength it takes to save myself from quicksand
I move deliberately to be rid of the thick muck that holds me down
I am saving my own life, one discarded thought at a time.
This is not a journey for the weak.

All Is Well

Come to me, all who would hear
I have wonderful news to share
And it is this:
It does not matter
Whatever concerns you
Whatever makes you afraid to get out of bed in the morning
Whatever makes you strap on your armor.
Wait—just a minute
Take a deep breath—3, 4
You do not even need to count to 10
Before you feel the calmness of The Great One
Who has your back
Who Loves you beyond any and all that THEY say or do
And knowing that
THEY becomes they
And what is left is
The Great One
Loving you to Peace
And all is well

Finding My Voice

Finding my voice came later in life…
after I gave up finding my "savior"--
the one who would "get me" and always love me.
On that long and disappointing search,
I kept running into rules
that constricted who I was.
And who was I anyway?
If I didn't know
how could my saviors know?
I took off my masks one by one
and got to work saving myself.
With eyes wide open, I began to ask:
"What do I think?"…
and I paid attention!
Which led to discerning my truth
Which led to accepting myself
Which led to trusting myself
Which led to loving myself
Which led to finding my voice.
And now here I AM
What's next?

The Road To Perfection

The road to perfection is not what you may think.
It's not about how you look, how you perform,
or how much money you have.
It's about how you connect to God
Perfection is pinpoint focus on the One Power.
ALL that is.
And all else follows.
To *BE* perfection all false ideas fall away
Because you no longer give them attention
And you stand unadorned with an unspeakable beauty
In the light of God's love flowing through you
And out into the world.

Drifting

Drifting…drifting…
Sometimes floating along with no purpose
Sometimes slamming into the mountainside with no brakes
When I let go of my grip on the steering wheel
It popped off!
Is this what it means to be reborn?
Is this how I build trust in God?
My ego is shrinking---slowly
This will be a long trip.
I feel it baring its teeth
--jaws in a death grip
Stop it! Let go of me!
You do not have permission!
I did not come this far to stop.
I Will Not Stop
Drifting is not the same as coasting
Right now—drifting is just where I am
On this trip to somewhere beautiful.

Taming Ego

Taming my ego is like
Cutting the tag off of my pillow
Sometimes I just want to rip it off
But it won't rip without tearing the pillow
And so I cut with my surgical shears
One small piece at a time.
I like seeing the flap that I've created.
It's getting longer as I am getting lighter
I'm proudly happy—happily proud
Of my emancipation from the imagined consequences
Of removing that tag.

Inner Voice

Which inner voice will you listen to today?
The indignant driver who was cut off?
The frightened child who is still nursing hurts?
The jilted lover who was lied to?
Or the perfectly efficient adult who can't tolerate the imperfection of others?
Why not the voice of GOD?
The voice of LOVE
No Matter What
You don't have to have the answers—
Just respond with love
With a look, a hug, or a kind act or word
Or silence
From the heart, not the head.

Walking in the Woods

While walking in the woods today
I had many thoughts.
Careful! Don't step on the rain-slick rocks
Stay on the path—there are chiggers and ticks.
Stop! Enough!
I recognize you!
Connecting to the Christ-God within me I say:
Peace. Be Still.
Body, Be Peace
And, I was.
I continued my walk
And smiled to myself when I slipped again

Out of My Comfort Zone

Shaking things up
Taking a Risk
Daring to Leap.
Birds aren't given a choice when they are pushed from the nest
It's do or die, and then they fly.
Surely I can take a road trip by myself
Just me and my GPS
To places I've never been
Making decisions I've never made
Ahh… The expansiveness of it all!
Checking fears and putting them to bed
As I go bravely onto the interstate.

Different But Equal

Take away the pedestal----
I no longer want or need it.
I stand barefoot on the ground
shoulder to shoulder with my sisters and brothers
Different, but equal
Respectfully acknowledging our individual journeys,
our individual truths.
Lending a hand when possible
Opening my heart always
Seeing beyond the physical
To the love that connects us all.
Having patience with this boot camp that we call
Human Experience.

Creativity

Creativity …
Can be Joy expressing itself.
Bubbling over your pen, brush, clothing…
whatever you wish.
No holds, no restrictions
Pure love expressing itself
Or, It *Can* be dark.
Guilt-ridden
Small-making
Which will you choose?
Become as a little child, expressing pure joy
uninhibited by human rules and laws tamping you down
Be the rainbow in other's lives
Refuse to be stomped on by well-meaning others.
Lead the way for those who have lost sight of their rainbows.

This is So Much Fun!

How often do you say that?
Don't you want to live that way?
Whatever it is---
Jump in!
Get your hands dirty--
your fingernails split and broken
Wholehearted participation!
Stop caring about how you look to others.
Their approval is not a part of your fun.
Their disapproval is not a part of your fun.
Your fun belongs to you.
Seize it! Let it take you on
Adventure, after Adventure, after Adventure
Send postcards.

Joyful Dreaming

Magical, unlimited, delightful, pure joy
There is no room for shadows in my dreams
Only dancing and leaping and twirling until my head spins
And I dissolve into laughter that brings laughter to others
The kind of laughter of children chortling over some silly thing
that tickles them delightfully
The kind of laughter that comes from deep down and holds on
until you've cleansed your body of all that fears
The kind of laughter that washes over everywhere you are standing
and spreads forth to your neighbors and makes everyone happy
Ahh…What Bliss!
What a wonderful shared moment.
Not the fake TV commercial kind
But a true shared moment of connection
When you see the beauty in everyone
And you know what heaven is.

Happy Place

I am in a happy, grateful place
and I want to share it with you.
To bring you right into this circle of light
and watch you smile.
Smile with your lips, your eyes, your loose and relaxed shoulders.
Thank you for coming.
We really should do this more often.

Feelings of Joy

Feelings of Joy too big to be expressed in words
can only be felt
by standing still and letting them wash over you.
They carry you away from that spot where you were standing
and bring you to a grander place
And your expanded self wants to share
<u>Has</u> to share
Or you'll burst
So you reach out and become the spark that finds another
And so it goes.

Loving You

I look at you with Loving eyes
And see only perfection
I hear your voice in its anger and shame
And hear only perfection
I touch your rigid body in a Loving hug
And feel only perfection
I sense your fears and how they drive your life
And know only perfection
Oh, if only you would know it too.

I Choose

I do understand that there is a time for everything
And that with understanding, everything becomes more of everything
And I know that we can choose where we put our attention.
So here is what I choose:
I choose to love you.
And to show it—I will listen to you
And while listening, I will continue to love you
And our love field will expand
And if you love me back…
Whoa! We may have to wear weighted shoes.

We Breathe the Same Air

When you get clearer—see who you really are,
It helps me.
I breathe it in.
When I throw off false beliefs and expand my understanding
It helps you.
You breathe it in.
Let's agree to help each other through life
And in doing so,
Help others too.

Talk to Me

Talk to me
Tell me what you know
Don't make me dig it out
one uninformed question at a time,
Like some deeply buried treasure from an ancient civilization.
What is your silence saying about your belief in me? In yourself?
I can't know; and guessing is futile.
Truth *does* set you free from the bonds that hold you in "stuck".
Fears can be overcome
Light shines brightly
and illuminates the path that you could not see.
I have my best walking shoes on
and am prepared to go the distance with you.
Talk to me.

Stepping Back

How can I show love
when you expect me to fail?
How can we connect
when everything I do is wrong?
I don't want to be your scapegoat—
the one who enables you to divert your task of going within
to reveal your shadows

That has been my role.
I see the pattern and I am breaking it.
I will step back, step aside,
and allow you to walk that road by yourself;
Hoping it brings you to a place of self love
where we can have a conversation.

Look Me in the Eye

Look me in the eye
when you mumble under your breath.
Expose your feelings as they are happening
even when you don't want to suffer the consequences.
And I'll do the same for you.
It's how we grow and heal.
It's why we came together.

You Are Right

You are right.
I can't make you.
But oh, is it worth the win?
This immobile stance that has to be right?
Be willing to look at the internal hurts
that keep you from seeing what you are losing on your quest to be right.
Fingers white from gripping
Holding on to what does not serve you.
Hurt spreading beyond you.
I cannot…will not…
Be a part of this.
With sadness, I release our bond.

Freedom

What does freedom mean to me?
That I am free to choose and accept the responsibility for my choice
Free to choose again, and again, and again to reach a new place--
as I discover and express who I *really* am.
Free to breathe without feeling a restriction in my chest
or fear of others' reprisal

How do we live in a space where we recognize that we *all*
have that same freedom?
We do it one brave soul at a time.
Go in; Go in deeper, deeper, Brave One
Into the depths of your heart where only you know the feelings.
Breathe with your feelings
Allow them to circulate… Be free… Move about
Then ask them to come forward
One by one
to talk to you.
Stay deep within your heart, where it's safe to be you
as you become a loving parent to your feelings--
The kind of parent who is always there for you.

Look with Love upon your children
Do they make you proud? Joyful?
or do you cringe at their intensity, logic, or lack of?
Talk to each of them as they come forward,
knowing that they may simply need to understand in a different light
Or they may *really* need to express themselves—
their hurt and their fear bubbling over
And then love them more and more and forever again
as you hold them in your heart.
Each part of you is precious.
Each aspect has something to teach
It is for you to decide which is the You as You want to BE
and which needs more love, more understanding.
That is Freedom
You get to decide.
You have the responsibility to decide.
And now, you have become an expanded version of YOU.
REPEAT

A Declaration of Love

I am so touched
By my beautiful soul
And the many storms it has weathered.
And yet it still stands
Steadfast and strong,
Battered around the edges,
Resilient in the middle.
A beautiful testimony to all that it has experienced.
I honor you Dear Soul!
You are like a loving grandparent to me;
and have now allowed me to be a loving grandparent to you.
One who always has time to listen and hear;
One who never rushes you through things
Or pushes you to be a certain way.
One who is patient and kind and exudes
Love for *me.*

We have fought battles to be here---
Slayed dragons; awakened sleeping princesses
to arrive where we live in gentle peace.
We have re-created our world in one lifetime:
Our metamorphosis has come together.
I honor you.
I love you.
I am so grateful for you.
And we are just getting started.

www.ingramcontent.com/pod-product-compliance
Lightning Source LLC
Chambersburg PA
CBHW071321080526
44587CB00018B/3307